I0457973

NOT
ABOUT
NOTHING

Hakim Ibn Adam

Copyright © 2025 Three Roses Publishing

All rights reserved. No part of this book may be reproduced, distributed, or transmitted in any form or by any means, including photocopying, recording, or other electronic or mechanical methods, without the prior written permission of the publisher, except in the case of brief quotations embodied in critical reviews and certain other noncommercial uses permitted by copyright law.

Threerosespublishing.com

ISBN: 978-1-9990656-9-0

DEDICATION

To the one who taught

silence.

Contents

I

The lake is glass. No wind. Early autumn. The
leaves have not yet decided. He came to think
about nothing, but nothing keeps turning into
everything. Nothing was supposed to mean:
peace. Nothing was supposed to mean: no
thoughts of the choices made. Instead,
nothing became a mirror, and in the mirror,
he sees every choice he thought was free.

He sees his younger self standing at the airport
with one suitcase.

His mother is crying but trying not to. She is

crying because she knows what he does not: he will come back, but will not return. The person who boards this plane is her son. The person who steps off at the other end will be someone who remembers being her son.

His father's hand is on his shoulder—too heavy, saying nothing. In his silence is everything he learned from his father: men leave, this is necessary, this is what breaks the world and makes it.

Hakim thinks he was leaving for two years, maybe three. He will finish the degree, learn what cannot be learned here, come home with the knowledge that will save—what? The family, the country, himself? He doesn't know yet that these are different things, mutually exclusive, all impossible.

The loudspeaker announces his flight in a language that is not his mother tongue. She hears it, she knows what it means.

Forty years later, by the lake, he understands what his mother understood.

The self is not portable. You cannot pack it in a suitcase, carry it across oceans, set it down unchanged. The process of leaving is the process of becoming different. You cannot step outside the world to move through it. Every crossing changes what crosses.

He thought he was choosing freely—the scholarship, the degree, the future that could not be built in the old country.

He thought freedom meant: I decide. What he

learned: freedom means deciding within a web of relations you did not choose and cannot escape.

His mother's tears, his father's silence, and what made leaving necessary and made staying impossible—these were not external to his choice. They were the substance of it.

All true. All verified by the departure, the exile, the years of becoming someone his mother would not recognize.

The lake ripples faintly, as if the past exhaled.

The sky holds its reflection, and the reflection holds him—a man remembering that the first step is also the fracture.

II

The lake reflects nothing but sky, emptiness mirroring emptiness. He gazes into the absence and sees the first wound of belonging.

He sees the first time someone asks him to explain. Not where he is from—that comes later, always—but to explain why. Why do his people do this? Why do they believe that? Why their history bends toward flame?

As if millions of people share one mind, and he holds the key. As if one mouth could translate centuries of disagreement.

He opens his mouth and becomes a translator. Not of words but of worlds. He simplifies, flattens, and makes digestible what cannot be digested. He removes the contradictions, the centuries, the arguments his grandfather had with his father. He gives them what they can hold.

This is when he learns: to exist here, he must become less. Not cruelly. Not with malice. But with the patient erosion of being asked to explain until explaining becomes breathing, until he can no longer speak without first translating himself into something they can recognize.

He does not say: I am as confused as you are. I do not speak for anyone but myself, and barely that.

He says what will end the question. This, too, is a departure.

By the lake, he remembers the exhaustion. The constant work of being legible. Of making himself smaller so he could fit through doorways built for different shapes.

He became fluent in reduction. This is what assimilation means: not joining, but subtracting until you are simple enough to be permitted. You do not bring your whole self. You bring the version that does not require explanation.

The self that left the airport was whole. Complicated. Contradictory. The self that learned to explain became coherent. Singular.

False.

He thought this was survival. Perhaps it was. Perhaps survival and betrayal are sometimes the same word.

By the lake, the silence deepens. It presses against his skin, like memory made liquid.

He whispers: "I have become fluent in erasure."

The lake answers—not with echo, but with reflection, the most merciful form of silence.

III

The lake holds its breath. A leaf falls—one syllable of autumn, breaking the skin of stillness. He closes his eyes and sees—

The fluorescent light of the laboratory. The hum of centrifuges. He is twenty-seven and has found what he came for: a world that makes sense. Molecular biology. Where everything reduces to sequences, to proteins folding in predictable geometries, to mechanisms that can be mapped and understood.

Here, finally, no one asks him to explain his people. No one wants him to translate centuries. Here, there is only DNA, RNA, the elegant simplicity of base pairs. Here, he is not representative of anything except his data.

He pipettes carefully. Measures precisely. The organism on the slide—a nematode, transparent, simple—contains in its genome the same basic machinery as every living thing. Reduce it far enough, and there is no mystery, only chemistry. This is what science promises: clarity purchased through reduction. Break the complex into components. Map the components. Understand.

It is beautiful. He believes this. The

reductionist method works. He can predict, manipulate, and control. When he submits his first paper, the reviewers do not care where he was born or what language his mother speaks. They care only whether his methods are sound, his data clear, and his conclusions are justified.

This is freedom, he thinks. This is what he came for.

His advisor is pleased. "You have a gift for this," he says. "For seeing through the complexity to what's essential."

He does not tell him he has been practicing this his whole adult life. Reduction as survival. Simplification as a passage. He has learned to see through himself the same way he sees through the nematode—strip away the complications, find the basic machinery, make it legible.

At night, sometimes, he remembers his grandfather. A poet, a mystic. A man who spent his life contemplating the divine names, the infinite attributes, the inexhaustible mystery.

His grandfather would have looked at the nematode and seen not a mechanism but a miracle. Would have insisted that the whole is more than its parts, that life cannot be reduced without being destroyed.

But his grandfather never published in peer-reviewed journals. Never secured funding. Never built a career in a country that had no place for him.

Science gave him what mysticism could not: a method, a language, a community that judged him by his work alone.

He thought he was choosing the truth. Perhaps he was. Perhaps truth has more than one face, and he could only afford to look at one.

By the lake, he sees the pattern. He became fluent in two kinds of reduction: the cultural and the methodological. Both promised the same thing—acceptance purchased through simplification. Make yourself simple. Make the world simple. Then you can be understood. Then you can understand.

It worked. He published. He built a career. He

belonged to a community that cared nothing for where he came from, only where his research led.

But at what cost? His grandfather's mystery, dismissed as unscientific. The holistic vision, sacrificed for measurable parts. He learned to see organisms as machines and himself as a mechanism. Clean. Precise. Reducible.

The nematode cannot be reduced without being destroyed. Neither can a person. Neither can a tradition. But reduction was the price of entry, and he paid it twice—once with his culture, once with his epistemology.

He thought science would save him from having to translate. Instead, it taught him to translate everything—life into chemistry, experience into data, mystery into mechanism.

Both translations were betrayals. Both were necessary. Both were insufficient.

This is what he could not see then: that the method which freed him from one prison was building another. That clarity purchased through reduction is not the same as understanding. That what you abandon shapes what you become as much as what you keep.

By the lake, he watches the ripples spread—the water thinking itself outward. He understands: Every method is a confession. Every clarity, a wound. Every reduction, an attempt to bear the unbearable abundance of the Real.

IV

The ripples spread outward from where the leaf touched the surface. Wider, fainter, until they reach the edges and disappear. The lake tries to return to stillness, but the wind has begun. Small disturbances across the water. He sees—

He is thirty-one when he marries. She is kind, intelligent, and grew up here. She wants to know him. He tries to let her. But being known requires being present in ways he has learned to avoid. It requires not translating, not reducing, simply being, and he has forgotten how.

Or perhaps he never learned. Perhaps the young man who left the airport was already preparing for a life lived in solitude, and all the years of attempted connection were the detour, not the destination.

She asks him what he's thinking. Often. He learns to have answers ready—simple thoughts, explicable thoughts. The truth is: he is thinking in layers she cannot access, in language that has no translation, in references to a grandfather's poetry and a nematode's transparent simplicity and the space between them where something wordless lives.

He loves her. This is true. But love across any

divide requires constant work. Not the work of affection but the work of making yourself available, of existing in the shared world rather than the interior one, of participating in domesticity when participation for him means something else entirely.

They have daughters. He is present. He is a good father. He watches them grow into people who will never fully know where he came from because he cannot fully explain it. He gives them what he can—stories, values, fragments of a tradition that cannot survive translation intact.

But he is also always slightly elsewhere. In the place where thought happens without mediation, where reality can be engaged without first making it legible to another.

She eventually stops asking what he's thinking. This is when the marriage becomes easier. When she accepts that part of him is permanently elsewhere. When solitude is permitted even within togetherness.

This is not failure. They build a good life. But it is built on the understanding that he cannot be fully present in the way a partnership promises. Cannot bring all of himself into the shared space. Cannot stop translating long enough to simply be with another.

By the lake, he understands: the loss was not of intimacy but of the illusion that intimacy completes you. That being known by another is necessary. That participation requires witnesses.

The mystic withdraws not from reality but into deeper reality. Solitude is not absence. It is presence without mediation.

Here, by the lake, alone, he participates more fully than he ever could through the exhausting work of translation that every human relationship requires.

This is not loneliness. Loneliness is wanting connection and lacking it. This is something else—the recognition that the deepest engagement happens in silence, in solitude, in the space where you do not have to explain yourself into existence.

All the departures, all the reductions, were preparing him for this. Not teaching him to be alone because he failed at being together, but teaching him that togetherness was never the destination. That some people are made for the interior journey, and all the years of trying to live otherwise were the detour.

V

The wind has changed. The lake darkens—

its surface rippled with small forgettings. He
sees—

His daughter is four when she asks him to
teach her. Not English—she already speaks it
better than he does, without accent, without
effort. She wants the other language. His
mother's language. The language he left
behind.

He tries. They sit together in the evenings. He
teaches her the words for simple things: bread,

water, sky. She repeats them carefully, her mouth forming shapes it was not built for. The sounds come out wrong, approximations, close but not quite.

He corrects her gently. She tries again. Gets closer. But there is something missing—the weight, the resonance, the centuries compressed into syllables. She is learning vocabulary, not a language. Words, not a world.

This is when Hakim understands: the transmission has failed. Not because he didn't try, but because what he carries cannot be carried forward. It belongs to a place, a time, a web of relations that no longer exists. His children are not extensions of his past. They are citizens of a different world.

He thought he could give them both. The heritage and the future. The language and the freedom from it. But these are not compatible gifts. To belong here fully, they must let go there fully. He knows this. He did the same thing.

The difference is: he remembers what he let go. They never had it to lose.

His daughter stops asking for lessons. She is twelve now, interested in other things. Sometimes she uses a word he taught her— usually wrong, but he doesn't correct her anymore. The language is dying with him. Or rather, it died when he left, and he has been carrying its ghost, hoping to pass it on, not understanding that ghosts cannot be inherited.

The lineage is broken.

What his grandfather gave his father, what his father gave him, ends here. His children will not pass it on because there is nothing left to pass.

By the lake, he understands: the loss was not of transmission but of the illusion that continuity is possible across rupture. That you can carry tradition through exile intact. That your children can inherit what you had to abandon to give them their lives.

The mystic's path is always solitary. It cannot be taught, only lived. He thought he could translate his grandfather's wisdom into

English, into molecules, into a philosophy his children could hold. But wisdom does not survive translation. It is not portable. It lives in the specific language, the specific place, the specific chain of teachers and students that has now been broken.

His children are free. Freer than he ever was. They do not carry the weight of elsewhere. They do not live between worlds. They are whole in a way he never learned to be.

Perhaps this is what he gave them: the freedom he purchased with his own fragmentation. Perhaps the tradition had to die so they could live.

Or perhaps he is simply consoling himself for what he could not prevent.

The lake listens. He does not speak again. The words have gone home to where sound begins.

VI

The wind is no longer gentle. The surface of
the lake breaks into small waves, choppy,
agitated. Clouds thicken overhead. He sees—

He is forty when his name becomes dangerous.

It happens overnight. One day, he is a
scientist, a colleague, and a neighbour. The
next day, he is from there. His name—the one
his father gave him, the one that means
"wise"—becomes a question. A suspicion. A
reason to look twice.

The images are on every screen. Buildings

falling. Bodies falling. And the men who did it—they use the same words his grandfather used. They claim the same God. They come from places not far from where he was born.

He watches from his living room. His wife beside him, hand over her mouth. On the television, the towers collapse again and again, replay after replay, until the horror becomes a loop, becomes background, becomes the new reality.

His phone rings. A colleague. "Are you watching this?" Yes. "My God." Yes. Silence on the line. Then: "You okay?" The question means: Are you safe? Or perhaps: Should I be worried about you?

He goes to work the next day because not

going would be worse. In the hallway, conversations stop when he approaches. Not obviously. Not cruelly. Just—a hesitation. Eyes that meet his and then look away. He understands: he has become representative again. Not of his data, not of his research, but of violence he did not commit.

In a meeting, someone says, "We need to understand why they hate us." Eyes turn to him. Not everyone. But enough. The old expectation: explain your people. But now with an edge. Now with fear underneath.

He opens his mouth. He has practiced this. Decades of translation, of simplification, of making the complex digestible. But this time the words catch. How does he explain that the men on the screen are not his people? That his grandfather's mysticism has nothing to do with their certainty?

Afterward, a younger colleague—someone he trained—approaches him carefully. "That must be hard for you." What must be hard? Having to explain, again, always, endlessly? None of it. He nods. Thanks him. Goes back to his lab where the nematodes, at least, do not care what his name means.

This is when he understands: distance does not protect. He thought by leaving, by building a life here, by raising children who speak without an accent—he thought he had transcended. But history is longer than distance. The past follows you across oceans.

And when violence erupts in the place you left, you carry its consequences whether you want to or not.

By the lake, the wind is cold now. The water dark. He understands: the loss was not of innocence but of the illusion that safety is possible. That you can leave history behind. That distance is the same as escape.

He thought he had built a sanctuary. A life where his name meant nothing but himself. But names carry weight beyond your choosing. They carry geography, history, violence committed by others in languages you share.

The mystic seeks solitude to escape the world's violence. But the world follows even into solitude. There is no outside. No distance far enough.

The wind breaks open the sky. The rain descends. Each drop, a marking of participation. Each ripple, a confession. He does not resist. He lets the rain erase his outline, lets the storm write him anew in the language of participation—where innocence ends, and understanding begins.

VII

The rain has found its rhythm. The lake no longer reflects—it receives. He sees—

He is fifty-five when he goes back.

His father is dying. The call comes in the middle of the night—a careful voice, speaking in the language he still understands but no longer thinks in. "You should come. Soon."

He books the flight. Tells his wife he will be gone a week, maybe two. She asks if she should come. He says no. This is something he needs to do alone. What he means is: he needs to see if he still belongs anywhere.

The airport is different. The city is different. Or perhaps they are the same, and he is what has changed. He takes a taxi through streets that were once as familiar as his own hands. Now they are—what? Not foreign. Not exactly. But not home either. Like looking at old photographs where you recognize the people but cannot remember being there.

He arrives at the family house. They embrace. Everyone is carrying the weight of staying. They sit together. Tea. Silence. They say, "You sound different". "I've been gone 30 years."

"Yes. We noticed."

This is not said unkindly. It is simply true. They noticed. They—the family, the place, the world he left—noticed his absence. And absence is a kind of presence, a shape cut out of the fabric.

His father is in bed, barely conscious. Hakim sits beside him, takes his hand. The old man's eyes open. Recognition, maybe. Or maybe just seeing a face, any face. He tries to speak. Hakim leans close. The words come in fragments, the old language, soft as prayer.

"You came back."

"Yes, father. I came back."

"Good. Good." A long pause. Then: "But you are not staying."

It is not a question.

Hakim sits with his father for three days. They do not speak much. What is there to say? The old man knows. Has always known. His son left and did not return. Came back, yes, but did not return. These are different things.

On the third day, his father dies. Quietly. As if he was waiting for permission.

His sisters give him papers to sign. The house. The last piece of ownership, of claim, signing it away. Making final what was already true. This, too, is a severance.

On his last day, he walks through the old neighbourhood. The mosque where his grandfather prayed is smaller than he remembered. The school is closed. The fig trees in the market are the same, or descendants of the same, bearing fruit for people who do not remember him.

He realizes: home is not a place you can return to. Home is a moment in time, and time does not reverse. The place still exists, but the moment is gone. His childhood, his family, his belonging—these happened here once, but they do not exist here now. They exist only in his memory, and memory is not a location. It is portable after all. He carries it with him. It lives nowhere but in him.

This is what return teaches: you cannot go back. You can only go to where back used to be.

By the lake, the rain is steady now. The water no longer reflects anything—the surface is too disturbed, too broken by impact.

He understands: the loss was not of home but

of the illusion that home is a place. That it waits for you. That it forgives your leaving by welcoming your return.

Home is not a place. It is a relation. And relations change. The people change. You change. The threads that bound you together loosen, fray, break. You can visit the location, but the relation is gone.

The mystic has no home. This is not a tragedy. This is a necessity. To see clearly, you must stand outside. But outside has no location. You cannot return to inside once you have learned to see from out here.

The philosopher has no home, because thought itself is the only homeland of the awake. There was no banishment. Only participation. Only the endless circulation of self, through self.

He thought he was exiled. But exile implies a home you can return to, a place you were cast out from. What he has learned: there was no casting out. There was only leaving, and staying left, and discovering that "there" and "here" are both words for elsewhere.

Perhaps this is what all the reductions were preparing him for. Not to find home but to accept homelessness. Not as a lack but as a condition.

The lake, like a patient mirror, holds it all—

the journey, the loss, the return that is not return, the endless becoming of what cannot arrive.

VIII

The rain withdraws. Light returns in fragments —shards upon the trembling lake.

Each glimmer is a thought surrendering its edge. The lake is not glass anymore. The surface moves, unsettled, carrying the memory of disturbance.

He is sixty-four when he finishes the work.

Years of thinking, writing, revising. The systematic philosophy: how consciousness arises within reality, not apart from it. How the observer and observed are mutually constituting. How being is relational, processual, and participatory. How everything connects to everything else in webs of relation that have no outside, no standing apart, no view from nowhere.

He doesn't know what he would work on next. What he couldn't say: I need to know if it was worth it.

The philosophy explains all of it. Why his mother's tears were not external to his choice, but the substance of it. Why assimilation required subtraction. Why science taught him to see through complexity to mechanism, and why that vision, while true, was insufficient. Why solitude became his mode of being. Why his children carry none of his weight and are freer for it. Why his name became dangerous and why distance did not protect him. Why home is not a place but a relation, and why all relations change.

The philosophy explains. But does it console? Does it offer peace?

The young man at the airport thought he was choosing knowledge that would save something. The family. The country. Himself. He was wrong on all counts. The knowledge did not save anything. It explained. Explanation is not salvation.

The philosophy says: all your choices led here necessarily. You could not have been other than what you became.

But necessity is not comfort. The philosophy

explains why his mother cried, but it does not dry her tears. It explains why the tradition died with him, but it does not resurrect it. It explains why he belongs nowhere completely, but it does not give him a home.

Would he choose this again, knowing what it cost?

The philosophy says: you did not choose. You participated in choosing. The choice chose itself through you, through circumstances, through relations you did not create but could not escape.

All the choices led here. To this lake, this moment, this recognition. The solitary man contemplating a life lived in fragments, understanding finally the pattern of the fragmentation, but not made whole by the understanding.

The mystic withdraws into deeper reality. But what if the deeper reality is just more clarity about how alone you are? What if participation, fully understood, means recognizing that you are connected to everything but at home in nothing?

Perhaps this is what he came to learn. That there is no final consolation. No moment when understanding makes the cost worthwhile. No philosophy that erases the tears, the broken lineage, the permanent displacement.

Perhaps the philosophy itself is what he made from the wreckage. Not compensation. Not justification. Just—the thing he could make. The only thing.

The lake is still now. Different from how it began, but still. The leaves have decided—some falling, some holding on a while longer. Autumn deepening. The season is turning.

He came to think about nothing. Nothing became everything. Everything became this: a man by a lake, understanding what his life cost and what it built, knowing that understanding is not the same as peace, but having no other answer.

Was it worth it?

He does not know. But he is still here. Still participating. Still engaged with reality in the only way he knows—through solitude, through thought, through the recognition that you cannot step outside to answer such questions. You can only continue. The choice continues choosing itself through you, and you call this living.

He does not need the answer anymore.

He has become the asking.

The question remains.

If he could go back, knowing everything,
Would he board that plane?

www.ingramcontent.com/pod-product-compliance
Lightning Source LLC
Chambersburg PA
CBHW020811130626
46554CB00006B/2379